A Route of Hope

Katie Ruth

A Route of Hope

Published in London by Abela Publishing Ltd.
Sandhurst, Berkshire, England

email Books@AbelaPublishing.com

www.AbelaPublishing.com/RouteofHope

ISBN 13: 978-0-9580584-3-0

First Edition, 2009

Acknowledgements

Photography

John Wood Photography

www.John-Wood-Photography.co.uk

--o--

Rev. Dr. Stephen Sizer

www.StephenSizer.com

10% of the net sale from this book

is donated to the Umthombo Street Children Charity

in Durban, South Africa

UMTHOMBO (Zulu): a wellspring

http://www.umthombo.org/

Dedication

To my family and friends

You carried me when I was weak

Encouraged me when I was low

And enlightened me when I was lost

Thank you so much

I will forever feel your arms around my heart

Contents

Share the love that's shown to us

every man a friend

because the love we have from God

is plenty and won't end

Introduction

You will keep in a perfect peace
him whose mind is steadfast,
because he trusts in You.
                    Isaiah 26:3

I find that many people in life are searching for excitement-
for new things that will send adrenaline round their bodies.
But for me, the most fantastic and joyful experience, has
been peace.

In 2005 after completing a degree in English Literature at
Sussex University, I moved back to my family home and
began work as a teaching assistant in a local school. The
transition from a very busy town like Brighton back to a
quiet village in Surrey was going to mean changes, but I
could never have expected or anticipated how much my life
was about to change.

I was always a relaxed, confident, happy girl, with very little
to complain of.

In the autumn of 2005, I fainted one day on the floor of my
family's kitchen. My mother said that she caught me and

that I did not bang my head when I fell, but I woke up with about two years' memory loss.

I had to be reintroduced to my boyfriend's family, even though I had just returned from spending a lovely holiday with them in France.

In the following weeks I developed panic disorder.

I saw many great doctors in London but they were unable to offer me a cause of my problem.

Subsequently, I have learned that panic attacks are much more common than people think. I believe this may be because those who suffer are less able to communicate their feelings well. I spent 18 months having panic attacks every day. The first six months of it was constant painful anxiety.

During this time, I was disabled from doing the 'normal' things in life I previously enjoyed. The only things I was able to do, while suffering with panic attacks, was cooking, playing card games, watching episodes of 'Friends' and writing poetry. These poems are a reflection of my observations and feelings about life from my new perspective on topics such as friendship, feeling at home, and God's gorgeous artistic designs.

When the relaxed 'me', transformed into the very anxious, panicky 'me,' I felt like I had completely lost the plot! But the one thing which may sound crazy…is that I am very grateful to God for the experience. I am glad that this happened to me.

My favourite bible verse, which gave me immense hope and comfort throughout my experience, is from the start of the book of James…

"Consider it pure joy, my brothers and sisters, whenever you face trials of many kinds, because you know that the testing of your faith produces perseverance. Let perseverance finish its work so that you may be mature and complete, not lacking anything."

(T.N.I.V James 1, verse 2-4)

These two years were indeed a 'trial' for me, and felt almost unbearable, but were in actual fact a huge benefit to me. God answered my prayers in such special ways and showed me so many miracles. He taught me lessons which have completely changed my outlook on life.

My doctors told me that I recovered from the disorder like I had sprinted a marathon. But I thought two years of painful anxiety seemed far too long, until I met people who have suffered in similar ways for decades.

For those of you who do not have experiences of panic attacks; for me, it felt like this: even though you may know very well that you have absolutely nothing to fear or worry about, you are suddenly overwhelmed by adrenaline pumping round your body, which means you are shaking, feeling the need to vomit, and frightened as if you feel someone has a gun pointed against your head. This sudden distress combined with the upset of knowing it is due to a mental illness, accelerates the confusion and terror.

One thing which I must pass on, was advice from a therapist which made a massive difference for me in my ability to control and minimalise panic attacks. If you panic, look at a clock or watch and spend five seconds taking in a long and slow deep breath. Five seconds breathing in and five seconds breathing out is the ten second breathing cycle and when repeated twice, just twenty seconds of breathing slowly, halves your heart rate. Spending a few minutes each day practising this slow deep breathing method was extremely helpful to me. Even if it's hard to measure any difference on a day to day basis, you will be able to see steps towards recovery in a matter of weeks or months. This may

4

sound crazy to anyone with no experience of anxiety; but when you recover and begin to feel deeply peaceful relaxation, it is an extremely exciting experience!

I was brought up in a Christian family, and my father is a vicar. But it wasn't until I began to feel so poorly that I knew for sure that God is real. The realisation that eternity in paradise is actually going to happen is indescribable! I collected quotations and phrases from many people who inspired and comforted me when I was sick, and my favourite (which I think will always put a huge smile on my face!) is from C.S. Lewis, "Joy is a serious business in Heaven!"

My second favourite which I'm slightly embarrassed to admit but which my friends will smile at, was on a postcard which I felt summed up my years of anxiety, cooking too much (becoming a chocoholic!) and playing with words. The postcard showed a picture of a lady holding a big chocolate cake and smiling while saying 'Stressed… is desserts spelled backwards!'

I believe that my speedy recovery is a result of many things which are all fantastic gifts from God. My therapy from Jan Gooding and Peter Wilson was awesome. Thank you two so much, you are lifesavers!!! God provided me with the most loving, supportive, and devoted family and friends whom I treasure for their aid in comforting me. But the other lifesaver, the one I owe everything to, is Jesus.

Through my disorder I learned that guilt and shame can be in many cases the most painful feelings for people to cope with. But understanding fully the forgiveness that Jesus brings us through the sacrifice of His life, enables us to experience the complete loss of all guilt and shame, and brings the real deep peace that I have been so excited and relieved by. When I recovered, I was baptised to start my life again in Christ. The wisdom and guidance that God showed me has changed all my aspirations, motivations, goals and intentions for a terrific new route towards Him.

I have been so moved by an experience of feeling my life torn apart, and rebuilt with God's pure love. Pure love has been the most amazing thing to learn of. That no matter where you are, what you do or what you look like, there is a very powerful and pure, loving hand holding you. I watched an Indiana Jones film recently where they searched for treasures and had the biggest smile on my face afterwards while thinking that the greatest treasure in existence is God's love for us, and that we are all invited to 100% of it!

I am very grateful to God for the gift of photography. I have been happily remembering all my lovely memories with family and friends who gave much of their time helping me regain my memory loss. But the one memory which was very precious to me, my friend Katherine reminded me of, was that shortly before the faint which began this hard trial, I had prayed and asked God to prove himself to me. So I think I asked for it! (I try to pray rather carefully these days!)

God has answered my prayers very kindly and clearly in recent years. It was my biggest childhood dream to write a book, but I never thought I would be able to aim for that. After my years of panic I had accumulated a collection of about 50 poems and did not know whether to type them up and save them or to throw them away. When I started typing one, I shook with panic and so could not type. I prayed that night that God would give me a clear sign if I should share my poems or throw them away. It could not have been clearer to me when I was contacted by the publishing industry the very next day with great encouragements that I should be published! God made my favourite dream into the reality you now hold in front of you. After reading my poems you may agree with me that it's a special miracle! ☺

While studying Psychology at A Level, I remember learning of the importance of expressing oneself. My poems are exactly that. They are in no way an attempt to be clever, creative or sophisticated in the use of our language. When I have felt overwhelmingly full of emotions, I have grabbed a pen, and the poems have flowed out of me like sneezing on a page! But I hope that they bring you a glimpse of the comfort, direction, and pure love that God has blessed me with.

It really is worth climbing that huge mountain of an obstacle in order to see the beautiful view that God has made for you to enjoy and share with Him.

Thank you for your time.

God bless,

Katie

"The gift of writing enabled her to track a route of hope on the journey to recovery."

(Katie's mother, 2009)

Nature

 Leaves

Every single leaf only compliments the next

Differing in colour, body shape and neck

Some delight the eyes, fingers and nose

Shimmering, modest, reaching or enclosed

Our Lord made each one unique

Sunshine and water, little do they seek

But they bring us pleasure, beauty, comfort too

A mass of green carpet, little drops of dew

Always fresh, gentle and alive

Peaceful, calm, only growth to strive

I feel so very lucky, gazing at my view

Clear perfect beauty, I'd like to share with you.

"On each side of the river stood the tree of life, bearing twelve crops of fruit, yielding its fruit every month. And the leaves of the tree are for the healing of the nations."
(Revelation 22:1-2)

Stars

Tonight, can you count the stars, as they blink at you?

They may seem like thousands, or maybe just a few

The big ones and the small, the yellow and the white

You may see throughout the day, but mostly just at night

Sometimes they will sparkle, while shining down on you

Like they are reflecting all the good you do

Our Lord gave us the stars and shows us there is light,

No matter where; we are reminded of his might.

"Those who are wise will shine like the brightness of the heavens, and those who lead many to righteousness, like the stars for ever and ever."
(Daniel 12:3)

The Lake

My View; a hundred shades of just one colour; green

An empty blue sky, peaceful as a dream

Surely God created, no one else could make

Beauty of this scale; the sun reflecting lake.

The surface, shimmering, like ripples made of glass

It makes the grasses emerald and earth beneath like brass

Nature living calm, seeming heavenly

Only hearing birds, squirrels and the bee.

Swans glide as though forever is today

Circle undisturbed, no one in their way.

And the Valley Gardens, famous is this land

Shrubs and flowering trees, unique and so grand.

Very well maintained so the life can grow

In this special place, much beauty to show.

The Totem Pole is high, a precious work of art

Brightening the entrance, where this walk can start

But I began where the lake flies to fall

Moving over rocks, becomes not flat, but tall

There's much to see around Virginia Water Lake

Thankfully, a gift, we are all free to take.

By Ruchia Bundy

After the Rain

Diamonds on the leaves

They're perfectly round

The blue sky is settled

And there's much less sound

The grass is looking happy

Waving to the trees

Where the birds are sitting

In the evening breeze

And the flowers are thankful

That now they can show

Their beautiful colours

Early, tomorrow.

"Never again will the waters become a flood to destroy all life. Whenever the rainbow appears in the clouds, I will see it and remember the everlasting covenant between God and all living creatures of every kind on the earth." (Genesis 9:15-16)

Struggles

Typique de Moi

I haven't done the washing up
I haven't fed the cat
I've got that wedding next weekend
And haven't bought a hat!
Procrastination
Should be my middle name
I want to improve
But every day's the same.
I haven't done the paperwork
My desk is piling high
But all I want to do is sit
And gaze up at the sky.
Should I tell my doctor
I have low energy
Or just perhaps
Am I lazy?
We all have potential
So what is mine?
I should try my best
That will be fine.

"Go to the ant, you sluggard; consider its ways and be wise!" (Proverbs 6:6)

Apart

The sunshine is beautiful

Here again today

But I feel cold

Because you are away

I miss you, friend

And hope you are well

I'm thinking of you, while gazing

Down a wishing well

My dreams are memories of

Before we were apart

You will always have a home

Here in my heart.

Hatred

Love, when you hate
Listen and wait
Give time to those
Who tread on your toes

Be a friend when someone
Causes you despair
Lend an open hand
When they're pulling out your hair

Exercise compassion
We all get it wrong
Sometimes or often
Don't make guilt last long

Because we're all forgiven
Every single sin
Show the love
Of this massive family we're in.

"You have heard that it was said, 'Love your neighbor and hate your enemy.'
But I tell you, love your enemies and pray for those who persecute you, that
you may be children of your Father in heaven." (Matthew 5:43-45)

Nightmare

The beauty of a nightmare

Is that when you wake

You realise your life

In fact, is not at stake!

Though you might remember

Feeling like you're sad

It's nice to start a morning

That is not so bad!

Appreciate the things you have

And the way you are

Start your day, and soon forget

Bad dreams don't leave a scar.

"Do not be anxious about anything, but in every situation, by prayer and petition, with thanksgiving, present your requests to God. And the peace of God, which transcends all understanding, will guard your hearts and your minds in Christ Jesus."
(Philippians 4:6-7)

Manipulated

Some people creep into your life, others bang

Like flavours mild, or spice with a tang

Along with you, like birds in the breeze

Or intertwined, ivy up trunks of trees

Some refresh you like a soft drink

Or like alcohol, blur how you think

The manipulative people we see

Sometimes change the way we want to be

Words heard from the people we love

Can move priorities we set above

Reflections of people seen in ourselves

Literature on our favourite shelves

See who walks along by your side

And don't be afraid to question your guide.

"Finally, brothers and sisters, whatever is true, whatever is noble, whatever is right, whatever is pure, whatever is lovely, whatever is admirable-if anything is excellent or praiseworthy-think about such things."
(Philippians 4:8)

Freedom from fear

Some may fear a wasp

Or a bumble bee

Strong winds or crashing waves

On a stormy sea.

Many fear disease

Loss of loved ones

Or the inevitable; aging

Here it comes.

But for a moment, try

Imagine no such things

As fearing pain or terror

Under angel wings

Everyday at peace
Constantly a smile
We will be with Jesus
In Heaven, in a while

There we'll stay forever
Perfect is this land
Open invitation
Just take His open hand

We'll look back remembering
Things on Earth we love
But no regrets and no fears
In our home above.

"The LORD is my light and my salvation- whom shall I fear? The LORD is the stronghold of my life- of whom shall I be afraid?" (Psalm 27:1)

Vanity

Please do not judge me on things like my hair

You know, the way you do, when you stop and stare.

I am not as vain, as I used to be

But I do not see this as a fault in me.

In fact I feel the different, like I have improved

Unlike you who needs 'special shoes' to be moved.

Please do not feel, that you have to judge

If you see on me, a small make-up smudge.

Please don't judge my bag, or the clothes I wear

Does it really matter if that; we don't share

If you want to judge me on things I've done or said

Then let's talk about it before we go to bed

Please do not let shallow things change how you see

I don't look as I used to, but I'm still me.

"Do not judge, and you will not be judged. Do not condemn, and you will not be condemned. Forgive, and you will be forgiven." (Luke 6:37)

Anger

A vicious circle; anger

Encourages itself

Hard to put away in

The mind, on a shelf

Punching walls

Will only hurt your hand

Don't let anger

Become so grand

Throwing something in the air

Will only land on you

Try concentrate on

Positive things to do

Calm, relax

And let anger leave

Let it be replaced by

Your heart on your sleeve.

"In your anger do not sin": Do not let the sun go down while you are still angry."
(Ephesians 4:26)

Lost

Lost... without direction

Which way shall I go?

Isn't this a journey that by now, I should know?

But every time I cross that bridge

And there is no more light

The feeling of confusion

Causes me a fright.

Thank you Lord, that every time

I feel like I'm alone

Every single time I'm lost

You bring me back home.

"we had to celebrate and be glad, because this brother of yours was dead and is alive again; he was lost and is found.' "
(Luke 15:32)

He has a plan

I need not feel like a disaster
God has plans for me
Even when my life feels like
A Catastrophe
Every struggle, each mistake
I now attempt to see
As part of my journey
Towards maturity
Everyday we can play
A part in God's plan
He has one for every child
Lady and each man
If we have faith and persevere
With Jesus as our guide
Joy, love and peace
God WILL provide.

"For I know the plans I have for you," declares the LORD, "plans to prosper you and not to harm you, plans to give you hope and a future."
(Jeremiah 29:11)

Feeling low?

Disliking oneself feels like a disease

Every criticism lingers to tease

Feeling you can't manage, too afraid to try

Letting each compliment pass, unheard, by.

Sure they didn't mean it, they are just kind.

Can anyone understand all that's in my mind?

Yes, I tell you now,

There's one who loves us all.

You may stumble, but, He will not let you fall.

God loves you, more than you could know

Let him comfort you, when you feel low.

God knows you better than you know yourself

Valuing you more than all of earthly wealth

You are very precious, uniquely made

Your own path to eternity is laid.

So let's take a step, God's love is all we need.

And it lasts forever. This is guaranteed!

"For you created my inmost being; you knit me together in my mother's womb. I praise you because I am fearfully and wonderfully made." (Psalm 139:13-14)

Mistakes

Please accept my 'sorry', a true apology
Love and kindness you would show, to forgive me.
Always hear perfection; no one here can be
Hard not to compare to role models we see
Obstacles we face, some so very high
With will and self esteem, we can only try.
Although the only thing that's perfect in the end
Is forgiveness from our Lord; to all a friend.
Encouragement and love, He guides us with a view
Knows what we will face, this I know is true
So we need not worry, what tomorrow brings
Because we can all glide on His outstretched wings
His hands hold us with comfort and eternal love
So let's enjoy this journey, 'til we join Him above.

"He will cover you with his feathers, and under his wings you will find refuge; his faithfulness will be your shield." (Psalm 91:4)

PURE LOVE

Jesus

The warm outstretched arms
When I need a cuddle
The clear explanation
When I'm in a muddle!

The cool clean water
Soothing a burn
Enthusiastic teacher
When I need to learn.

Caring and teaching
Guidance to the end
But here's the special bit;
Jesus is my friend!

By Rachel

Home

Home is not a roof
That shelters from the rain
Nor the same walls
We turn and see again

Home is not the silver
The brass or fireplace
Nor the kitchen table
Around; the pets we chase

Home is in our hearts
A place that sets us free
Allows us to relax
It's where we feel happy.

Consider not the hours
In a certain bed
Nor worry for the future
And where lies ahead

A caravan, a castle
A mansion or a shed
Could entertain a happy bunch
Sharing daily bread

Don't think of walls around you
Nor a roof above,
When you are surrounded
Just by those you love.

"Here I am! I stand at the door and knock. If anyone hears my voice and opens the door, I will come in and eat with them, and they with me."
(Revelation 3:20)

There for me

What beats an artist
Who can paint your dream
Or the friend who knows
Exactly what you mean
Nothing compares to
Feeling such a gain
Knowing your thoughts are shared
When you feel insane.
Both agreeing on
Your favourite game to play
Eager to learn
Each others new way
Able to share pain
Taking off the load
Share a destination
Take the same road
Always there for each other
As they can and will
I want to thank you Lord
For my friend, Phil.

"A friend loves at all times, and a brother is born for a time of adversity."
(Proverbs 17:17)

Friend

A lucky combination of beautiful and bright
I feel I'm with an angel, when you are in sight
You are full of love, peace, honesty
Thank you, for all that you have given me

A good friend nowadays is somebody who cares
Watches out for you, protects you and shares
After I have been with you, I feel like I'm strong
So I will try to be there when your days are long.

"One who has unreliable friends soon comes to ruin, but there is a friend who sticks closer than a brother." (Proverbs 18:24)

Family

Family, leaves on a tree

Places we can feel comfy

Similarity, or the same

Those who use a middle name

Those who are aware of shame

Yet full of love, all the same.

Such a love is elsewhere rare

But here is plenty, and we share

Nothing pushes us apart

Because we are adjoined in heart.

"Love does not delight in evil but rejoices with the truth. It always protects, always trusts, always hopes, always perseveres. Love never fails."
(1 Corinthians 13:6-8)

Waiting

Waiting for you here, now

Is just a pleasure

Our love is something

I could never measure

Our Lord has blessed me

With a blue sky

And comfortable seat

As trains pass by

The one that holds you

Brings me home a treasure

Thank you that your love

I'll never *need* to measure.

"But the fruit of the Spirit is love, joy, peace, patience, kindness, goodness, faithfulness, gentleness and self-control. Against such things there is no law."
(Galatians 5:22-23)

Warm Socks

What beats a pair of thick warm socks

When you're cold

What's better when alone

Than loving arms to hold

What beats a glass of water

When you're hot and thirst

Or hearing your name yelled with cheer

When you come first.

We thank those who support,

Comfort and provide

When you're lost, nothing beats

An excellent guide.

"The LORD is my shepherd, I lack nothing. He makes me lie down in green pastures, he leads me beside quiet waters, he refreshes my soul. He guides me along the right paths for his name's sake. Even though I walk through the darkest valley, I will fear no evil, for you are with me; your rod and your staff, they comfort me." (Psalm 23:1-4)

Love

There are many things in life that I really love,

I like to see as presents from God, who's above

Even little things, like chocolate and tea

Pictures of a mountain or views over sea.

Sometimes there are things, we feel we really need

Like alcohol and cigarettes or maybe books to read

Friends to say hello to, and give us a nice hug

Maybe draws and cupboards, or a fluffy rug!

I try to be so grateful for all that is around

All the natural colours, touch, smells and sound

Lord, I often wonder what it's like above

I know the most precious thing here with us, is love.

"And now these three remain: faith, hope and love. But the greatest of these is love."
(1 Corinthians 13:13)

Mum

Mum, I want to thank you
For all you are to me
Bringing me into
This awesome family.
Guiding, providing
Over many years
Always being there
To wipe away my tears.
You've taught me more than books
Could ever hope to show
So I have learned to sleep
And smile for tomorrow
I only dream of being
A mummy just like you
So with all my heart
And love, I say, Thank you!

Dad

Dad, your love is armour
For someone in a fight
Or when I feel blind
A sudden gift of sight.
When I've felt most lost
You've always been a guide
Never once in my life
Did you fail to provide.
So Many things you do in life
Make me proud of you
So with all my heart,
And love, I say, Thank you!

Perseverance

Perspective

On your warmest day

Somewhere else it's cold

Take something to buy

But for them, it's sold

Wipe dirt off a shoe,

For someone else, it's gold.

Some choose the different

Others use a mould

Some people guests,

You may feel at home

Even in a crowd

Some may be alone

Although on a train

You may sit and wait

You pass those on benches

At a fast rate!

The plane flies above you

Even faster still

Inside it may be warmer

But up there we would chill!

Things we watch on
The television screen
Are for some; non-fiction
Others; are a dream
Even those with vision
Sometimes feel blind
But everything we see
Is the way *we* find
My angle, perspective
May be far from you
And people may not see
As you want them to
But one thing, for sure,
Everywhere's the same,
That our God is love,
And Jesus is His name.

Rush

I really love to have a moment to spare
So many people rushing, I MUST be 'there'
Obsessed with destination, not so much 'the way'
Too fast to notice that they went astray.

Do you strive for your goal, no matter where it ends
Or take heed of redirection from a wise friend.

Stop for five minutes….or maybe more
Does it matter which town claims this floor?
Surely the journey is worth just the same
The in-between country also has a name.
Slow down a little, don't be scared to take
Time to reflect, and enjoy a break.

No Need

You don't need to see God, to know that He is there

Don't always have to give or take something, to share

You don't need to be an artist to make

To dream or imagine, to build or create

You don't need a pen to gather up your words,

Nor do you need telescopes to see there are birds

You don't always need to be tickled, to laugh

Or it to be the winter to wear a new scarf!

No need for perfection, for 'extremely good'!

It's only little seeds that grow into a wood

You don't need a medal to know that you can win

Or for an X-ray, to see what lies within.

"The heavens declare the glory of God; the skies proclaim the work of his hands."
(Psalm 19:1)

By Your Word

Please do guide me, Jesus
To live as You have shown
Living in Your love, Lord,
I'll not be alone.

The right things with my money
The right things with my time
The right things with my energy
Spent with You in mind.

To be a great example
To those who have not heard
So they can see your love in me,
Help me live by Your word.

Moving

Extremely happy pleasure

Can become like pain

The masses of the sea

From little drops of rain

The Earth keeps moving 'round

While we feel still

The sun is shining brightly

While we feel chill

Millions of people near

While we feel alone

People miles and miles apart

Talking on the phone

Muscles in the face

Warming of the heart

Some communication

And a love can start

Oldest memories

Solid like the rock

A time remains here with us,

Despite any clock.

"There is a time for everything, and a season for every activity under the heavens."
(Ecclesiastes 3:1)

Smile

I love to see a friendly face

Just to share a smile

It makes the journey pleasurable

For a while

The guy who helped the lady

Cross the busy road

Or carried her bags

Lightening her load

The child in the pushchair

Who just smiled at me

Made all my loneliness

Change into glee!

"The LORD bless you and keep you; the LORD make his face shine on you and be gracious to you; the LORD turn his face toward you and give you peace." '
(Numbers 6:24-25)

Sleep With Ease

Sometimes when you stare at one thing

Others disappear

You might try reaching out to find

It isn't quite so near

It might take blocking out your sight

To know that you could see

Or chains that hold you down

To realise that you were free.

Appreciate the things we have

Opportunities

We should grasp them with both hands

And then sleep with ease.

Share the love that's shown to us

Every man a friend

Because the love we have from God

Is plenty, and won't end.

See

Sometimes you don't see blue sky

Until the sun shines bright

Nor can you see cream colours

Until next to white

Sometimes you don't smell the air

Until the flowers grow

Or appreciate your height

Until you sink low

Can't treasure all the things we have

Until they're gone or moved

So let's see, thankfully,

And try show gratitude.

Celebration

Thank You

I want to say, thank you, Lord

For looking after me

Thank you for my friends

And my family

Thank you for the sunshine

That brightens up our days

And for all your love

You show in many ways

Thank you for our homes

We open with a key

And for all the fruit

We pick from the tree

Thank you for the teachers

Who guide us to know

And for the doctors

Who help us to grow

Thank you for the churches

That we can all go to,

So Lord, together

We can say, "Thank you!"

"give thanks in all circumstances; for this is God's will for you in Christ Jesus."
(1 Thessalonians 5:18)

Sport

It doesn't matter whereabouts you came from today

We have joined here just to share and play.

Our methods of practise may not be the same

But we enjoy the very same game.

Thank you for travelling to be with us here,

We hope you are motivated by our crowd's cheer!

You represent your home, these colours we'll not hide

Every single nation carries special pride.

Here, you are welcome, let our games begin!

Lord, please keep us safe, and let the best win.

Before Us

When I see the elderly
I smile and think 'well done!'
So many things you must have seen
So much you must have done.
I bet you're full of wisdom
Lessons you could share
It's a shame when young people
Fail to show they care.
You who built the roads
Each opportunity
That we may take for granted
You've made so much for me.
Traditions we enjoy
All that we now share
You who began this
I'm thankful you were there.
Even if your memory fails
To picture all you've seen
The smiles you've made
In our world
Mark where you have been.

Aim

How fortunate we are

When dreams become an aim

When what we have and what we want

Can then be the same.

Aims that were a dream

Once thought 'no can do'

Now in front, a straighter path

With a clear view.

Can't ignore what's ahead

When it gleams at you

What we just had faith in once,

Evidently true.

They will say 'try your best'

With all that you do

But choose an aim,

And with faith,

Enjoy, while you pursue.

"Forgetting what is behind and straining toward what is ahead. I press on toward the goal to win the prize for which God has called me heavenward in Christ Jesus." (Philippians 3:13-14)

Overwhelmed

I hope I continue to see beautiful and lovely things in our world.

But, I pray that I continue to be overwhelmed by them…

Like when I see nature, undisturbed

When I see love, felt and heard

When I see children learn to share

When I see peace between a pair

When I see courage and faith succeed

When I see growth from tiny seeds

When I hear birds singing to me

And when God's hands are holding me.

The way things were supposed to be

And how they will always be.

Hallelujah!

Baptism

I don't need to be perfect
To be loved by You
You built me and designed
All that I can do.
If I am content with
Where I am weak
Then Your love
Is all I have to seek.
It's not hard to find
Every single place
On this planet
Is full of your grace.
Opening my heart
Welcoming You in
Thank you SO much for
Forgiving all my sin
This day I start
Every day is new
Sweet Lord, here's to
Eternity with You!

"Yet to all who did receive him, to those who believed in his name, he gave the right to become children of God." (John 1:12)

Party

Christmas, birthday or your wedding day

Expectation, presents, certain things to say

People come together, traditions, to share

Organisation, how, when or where

Flowers, balloons, chocolate and treats

Gathering friends, family to greet

Some things don't matter, others mean a lot

Materialistic, what have I got?

One thing's the same, that is why we're here

Celebrate that those who we love are near.

"I tell you that in the same way there will be more rejoicing in heaven over one sinner who repents than over ninety-nine righteous persons who do not need to repent." (Luke 15:7)

You

There's no such thing as normal, average or the same
People may share hair colour, skin colour or name
God made us different, crafted us unique
Even little birds have different wings or beak
Everyone has different skills, things they love to do
So, no wonder we contrast in comparing views

People on a mountain may love to see ground flat
People in a storm, an umbrella or hat
Wishing rain would stop pouring down it seems,
While those in deserts, rain just in their dreams.

Some cultures strict, pressure to conform
Individuality traded for the norm
But we should celebrate how God made you 'You'
Appreciate the things that only **you** do
He gave you skills and talents, so let them grow
Sometimes, oneself; it's hard to get to know
When I pray for guidance, God reveals a way
A path I can then follow and try not to stray
Exercising things I feel in my heart, to do
So find the path, that's in your heart, which makes you just You.

"God created human beings in his own image, in the image of God he created them; male and female he created them…….God saw all that he had made, and it was very good." (Genesis 1:27 and 31)